THE
OF AUTHORITY
Scriptural Devotional

THE ATTITUDE
OF AUTHORITY

Scriptural Devotional

CARRIE PICKETT

Published in partnership between Andrew Wommack Ministries and Harrison House Publishers

Shippensburg, PA 17257

ISBN 13 TP: 978-1-6675-0463-6

ISBN 13 eBook: 978-1-6675-0464-3

For Worldwide Distribution, Printed in the U.S.A.

1 2 3 4 5 6 7 8 / 27 26 25 24 23

May you declare with boldness the promises of God in your life and to this world. May you stand firm knowing that greater is He that is in you, than he that is in the world!

Contents

Introduction

Greater is He that is in us than he that is in the world.

This truth should be a life-altering revelation that wakes you up each day with joy, boldness, and an attitude of victory! You are a child of God, filled with the fullness of the Godhead, and made complete in Christ!

You are redeemed, righteous and anointed. You have been positioned in Christ, who is over every principality and power. You have been equipped and commissioned with authority to preach the good news, cast out demons, and live supernaturally in this lost, natural world.

When we hide ourselves in the truth of the Word, we find the freedom that only truth can produce, and the boldness of knowing that every promise is backed up by heaven. As we believe—the impossible becomes possible! As we encounter any situation or trial, we can identify the lies of the enemy and resist with confidence. The victory already belongs to us! We can stand firm in faith, knowing that the enemy has been defeated by the work of the cross!

Having an attitude of authority is not based on your good works or deeds, but based on the truth that Christ lives in you, and He has given you authority over every situation and attack of the enemy.

Let the verses within this scriptural devotional stir up the revelation that you have been equipped and empowered by God Himself living in you. Resist the devil and he will flee!

Step out with boldness and begin living supernaturally!

Blessings and love,

Carrie Pickett

Boldness

Ephesians 3:8-13 NKJV

To me, who am less than the least of all the saints, this grace was given, that I should preach among the Gentiles the unsearchable riches of Christ, and to make all see what is the fellowship of the mystery, which from the beginning of the ages has been hidden in God who created all things through Jesus Christ; to the intent that now the manifold wisdom of God might be made known by the church to the principalities and powers in the heavenly places, according to the eternal purpose which He accomplished in Christ Jesus our Lord, in whom we have boldness and access with confidence through faith in Him. Therefore, I ask that you do not lose heart at my tribulations for you, which is your glory.

Acts 14:3 ESV

So, they remained for a long time, speaking boldly for the Lord, who bore witness to the word of his grace, granting signs and wonders to be done by their hands.

Proverbs 28:1 NIV

The wicked flee though no one pursues, but the righteous are as bold as a lion.

Acts 4:13 NKJV

Now when they saw the boldness of Peter and John, and perceived that they were uneducated and untrained men, they marveled. And they realized that they had been with Jesus.

2 Corinthians 3:12-17 NLT

Since this new way gives us such confidence, we can be very bold. We are not like Moses, who put a veil over his face so the people of Israel would not see the glory, even though it was destined to fade away. But the people's minds were hardened, and to this day whenever the old covenant is being read, the same veil covers their minds so they cannot understand the truth. And this veil can be removed only by believing in Christ. Yes, even today when they read Moses' writings, their hearts are covered with that veil, and they do not understand. But whenever someone turns to the Lord, the veil is taken away. For the Lord is the Spirit, and wherever the Spirit of the Lord is, there is freedom.

Acts 4:31 NLT

After this prayer, the meeting place shook, and they were all filled with the Holy Spirit. Then they preached the word of God with boldness.

Ephesians 6:19-20 NLT

And pray for me, too. Ask God to give me the right words so I can boldly explain God's mysterious plan that the Good News is for Jews and Gentiles alike. I am in chains now, still preaching this message as God's ambassador. So, pray that I will keep on speaking boldly for him, as I should.

Acts 4:29-30 ESV

And now, Lord, look upon their threats and grant to your servants to continue to speak your word with all boldness, while you stretch out your hand to heal, and signs and wonders are performed through the name of your holy servant Jesus.

Philippians 1:19-20 NKJV

For I know that this will turn out for my deliverance through your prayer and the supply of the Spirit of Jesus Christ, according to my earnest expectation and hope that in nothing I shall be ashamed, but with all boldness, as always, so now also Christ will be magnified in my body, whether by life or by death.

I Thessalonians 2:2 NKJV

But even after we had suffered before and were spitefully treated at Philippi, as you know, we were bold in our God to speak to you the gospel of God in much conflict.

Hebrews 4:16 KJV

Let us therefore come boldly unto the throne of grace, that we may obtain mercy, and find grace to help in time of need.

Philippians 1:14 AMP

Because of my chains [seeing that I am doing well and that God is accomplishing great things], most of the brothers have renewed confidence in the Lord, and have far more courage to speak the word of God [concerning salvation] without fear [of the consequences, seeing that God can work His good in all circumstances].

Acts 4:33 KJV

And with great power the apostles gave witness to the resurrection of the Lord Jesus: And great grace was upon them all.

Ephesians 3:12 NLT

Because of Christ and our faith in him, we can now come boldly and confidently into God's presence.

Acts 5:29-32 BSB

But Peter and the other apostles replied, "We must obey God rather than men. The God of our fathers raised up Jesus, whom you had killed by hanging Him on a tree. God exalted Him to His right hand as Prince and Savior, in order to grant repentance and forgiveness of sins to Israel. We are witnesses of these things, and so is the Holy Spirit, whom God has given to those who obey Him."

Attitude

Ephesians 4:23 AMP

And be continually renewed in the spirit of your mind [having a fresh, untarnished mental and spiritual attitude].

Philippians 3:12-15 AMP

Not that I have already obtained it [this goal of being Christlike] or have already been made perfect, but I actively press on so that I may take hold of that [perfection] for which Christ Jesus took hold of me and made me His own. Brothers and sisters, I do not consider that I have made it my own yet; but one thing I do: forgetting what lies behind and reaching forward to what lies ahead, I press on toward the goal to win the [heavenly] prize of the upward call of God in Christ Jesus. All of us who are mature [pursuing spiritual perfection] should have this attitude. And if in any respect you have a different attitude, that too God will make clear to you.

Numbers 14:24 NLT

But my servant Caleb has a different attitude than the others have. He has remained loyal to me, so I will bring him into the land he explored. His descendants will possess their full share of that land.

_____
_____
_____
_____
_____
_____
_____
_____
_____
_____
_____
_____
_____
_____
_____
_____
_____
_____
_____
_____
_____
_____
_____
_____

Romans 8:6 AMP

Now the mind of the flesh is death [both now and forever—because it pursues sin]; but the mind of the Spirit is life and peace [the spiritual well-being that comes from walking with God—both now and forever].

Psalm 115:1 ESV

Not to us, O LORD, not to us, but to your name give glory, for the sake of your steadfast love and your faithfulness!

Psalm 109:26-27 ESV

Help me, O LORD my God! Save me according to your steadfast love! Let them know that this is your hand; you, O LORD, have done it!

Psalm 109:21 BSB

But You, O GOD, the Lord, deal kindly with me for the sake of Your name; deliver me by the goodness of Your loving devotion.

Psalm 60:4-5 AMP

You have set up a banner for those who fear You [with awe-inspired reverence and submissive wonder—a banner to shield them from attack], a banner that may be displayed because of the truth. Selah. That Your beloved ones may be rescued, Save with Your right hand, and answer us.

Romans 8:28 KJV

And we know that all things work together for good to them that love God, to them who are the called according to his purpose.

Galatians 5:1 NKJV

Stand fast therefore in the liberty by which Christ has made us free, and do not be entangled again with a yoke of bondage.

Psalm 121:1-2 NLT

I look up to the mountains—does my help come from there? My help comes from the LORD, who made heaven and earth!

Psalm 142:7 ESV

Bring me out of prison, that I may give thanks to your name! The righteous will surround me, for you will deal bountifully with me.

Romans 8:37-39 NKJV

Yet in all these things we are more than conquerors through Him who loved us. For I am persuaded that neither death nor life, nor angels nor principalities nor powers, nor things present nor things to come, nor height nor depth, nor any other created thing, shall be able to separate us from the love of God which is in Christ Jesus our Lord.

Hebrews 11:1 NKJV

Now faith is the substance of things hoped for, the evidence of things not seen.

Psalm 29:11 NLT

The LORD gives his people strength. The LORD blesses them with peace.

Authority over Death

Psalm 118:17 NKJV

I shall not die, but live, and declare the works of the LORD.

Psalm 116:8-9 ESV

For you have delivered my soul from death, my eyes from tears, my feet from stumbling; I will walk before the LORD in the land of the living.

_____

_____

_____

_____

_____

_____

_____

_____

_____

_____

_____

_____

_____

_____

_____

_____

_____

_____

_____

_____

_____

_____

_____

Psalm 30:2-3 NKJV

O LORD my God, I cried out to You, And You healed me. O LORD, You brought my soul up from the grave; You have kept me alive, that I should not go down to the pit.

Psalm 33:18-19 ESV

Behold, the eye of the LORD is on those who fear him, on those who hope in his steadfast love, that he may deliver their soul from death and keep them alive in famine.

Psalm 124:1-5 KJV

If it had not been the LORD who was on our side, now may Israel say; If it had not been the LORD who was on our side when men rose up against us: Then they had swallowed us up quick when their wrath was kindled against us; Then the waters had overwhelmed us, the stream had gone over our soul; Then the proud waters had gone over our soul.

Hebrews 2:9 NKJV

But we see Jesus, who was made a little lower than the angels, for the suffering of death crowned with glory and honor, that He, by the grace of God, might taste death for everyone.

Hebrews 2:14 NLT

Because God's children are human beings—made of flesh and blood—the Son also became flesh and blood. For only as a human being could he die, and only by dying could he break the power of the devil, who had the power of death.

_____
_____
_____
_____
_____
_____
_____
_____
_____
_____
_____
_____
_____
_____
_____
_____
_____
_____
_____
_____
_____
_____
_____

The Work of the Holy Spirit with Your Authority

Acts 8:14-17 NKJV

Now when the apostles who were at Jerusalem heard that Samaria had received the word of God, they sent Peter and John to them, who, when they had come down, prayed for them that they might receive the Holy Spirit. For yet, He had fallen upon none of them. They had only been baptized in the name of the Lord Jesus. Then they laid hands on them, and they received the Holy Spirit.

Acts 1:8 KJV

But ye shall receive power, after that the Holy Ghost is come upon you: and ye shall be witnesses unto me both in Jerusalem, and in all Judaea, and in Samaria, and unto the uttermost part of the earth.

Acts 4:29-31 NKJV

"Now, Lord, look on their threats, and grant to Your servants that with all boldness they may speak Your word, by stretching out Your hand to heal, and that signs and wonders may be done through the name of Your holy Servant Jesus." And when they had prayed, the place where they were assembled together was shaken; and they were all filled with the Holy Spirit, and they spoke the word of God with boldness.

Acts 19:6-7 KJV

And when Paul had laid his hands upon them, the Holy Ghost came on them; and they spake with tongues, and prophesied. And all the men were about twelve.

Positioned in Authority

Psalm 18:31-40 BSB

For who is God besides the LORD? And who is the Rock except our God? It is God who arms me with strength and makes my way clear. He makes my feet like those of a deer and stations me upon the heights. He trains my hands for battle; my arms can bend a bow of bronze. You have given me Your shield of salvation; Your right hand upholds me, and Your gentleness exalts me. You broaden the path beneath me so that my ankles do not give way. I pursued my enemies and overtook them; I did not turn back until they were consumed. I crushed them so they could not rise; they have fallen under my feet. You have armed me with strength for battle; You have subdued my foes beneath me. You have made my enemies retreat before me; I put an end to those who hated me.

Psalm 20:7-8 KJV

Some trust in chariots, and some in horses, but we will remember the name of the LORD our God. They are brought down and fallen but we are risen and stand upright.

_____

_____

_____

_____

_____

_____

_____

_____

_____

_____

_____

_____

_____

_____

_____

_____

_____

_____

_____

_____

_____

_____

_____

Ephesians 6:14-18 AMP

So stand firm and hold your ground, having tightened the wide band of truth (personal integrity, moral courage) around your waist, and having put on the breastplate of righteousness (an upright heart), and having strapped on your feet the gospel of the peace in preparation [to face the enemy with firm-footed stability and the readiness produced by the good news]. Above all, lift up the [protective] shield of faith with which you can extinguish all the flaming arrows of the evil one. And take the helmet of salvation, and the sword of the Spirit, which is the Word of God. With all prayer and petition pray [with specific requests] at all times [on every occasion and in every season] in the Spirit, and with this in view, stay alert with all perseverance and petition [interceding in prayer] for all God's people.

Philippians 4:13 AMP

I can do all things [which He has called me to do] through Him who strengthens and empowers me [to fulfill His purpose—I am self-sufficient in Christ's sufficiency; I am ready for anything and equal to anything through Him who infuses me with inner strength and confident peace.]

Genesis 1:22-28 NKJV

And God blessed them, saying, "Be fruitful and multiply, and fill the waters in the seas, and let birds multiply on the earth." So, the evening and the morning were the fifth day. Then God said, "Let the earth bring forth the living creature according to its kind: cattle and creeping thing and beast of the earth, each according to its kind"; and it was so. And God made the beast of the earth according to its kind, cattle according to its kind, and everything that creeps on the earth according to its kind. And God saw that it was good. Then God said, "Let Us make man in Our image, according to Our likeness; let them have dominion over the fish of the sea, over the birds of the air, and over the cattle, over all the earth and over every creeping thing that creeps on the earth." So, God created man in His own image; in the image of God He created him; male and female He created them. Then God blessed them, and God said to them, "Be fruitful and multiply; fill the earth and subdue it; have dominion over the fish of the sea, over the birds of the air, and over every living thing that moves on the earth."

1 John 5:18 ESV

We know that everyone who has been born of God does not keep on sinning, but he who was born of God protects him, and the evil one does not touch him.

Acts 3:16 BSB

By faith in the name of Jesus, this man whom you see and know has been made strong. It is Jesus' name and the faith that comes through Him that has given him this complete healing in your presence.

Psalm 121:7-8 NKJV

The LORD shall preserve you from all evil; He shall preserve your soul. The LORD shall preserve your going out and your coming in from this time forth, and even forevermore.

_____
_____
_____
_____
_____
_____
_____
_____
_____
_____
_____
_____
_____
_____
_____
_____
_____
_____
_____
_____
_____
_____
_____
_____
_____

Psalm 124:8 KJV

Our help is in the name of the LORD, who made heaven and earth.

Psalm 144:1-2 ESV

Blessed be the LORD, my rock, who trains my hands for war, and my fingers for battle; He is my steadfast love and my fortress, my stronghold and my deliverer, my shield and he in whom I take refuge, who subdues peoples under me.

1 Corinthians 10:13 NKJV

No temptation has overtaken you except such as is common to man; but God is faithful, who will not allow you to be tempted beyond what you are able, but with the temptation will also make the way of escape, that you may be able to bear it.

2 Corinthians 4:18 AMP

So we look not at the things which are seen, but at the things which are unseen; for the things which are visible are temporal [just brief and fleeting], but the things which are invisible are everlasting and imperishable.

Ephesians 6:10-14 AMP

In conclusion, be strong in the Lord [draw your strength from Him and be empowered through your union with Him] and in the power of His [boundless] might. Put on the full armor of God [for His precepts are like the splendid armor of a heavily-armed soldier], so that you may be able to [successfully] stand up against all the schemes and the strategies and the deceits of the devil. For our struggle is not against flesh and blood [contending only with physical opponents], but against the rulers, against the powers, against the world forces of this [present] darkness, against the spiritual forces of wickedness in the heavenly (supernatural) places. Therefore, put on the complete armor of God, so that you will be able to [successfully] resist and stand your ground in the evil day [of danger], and having done everything [that the crisis demands], to stand firm [in your place, fully prepared, immovable, victorious]. So, stand firm and hold your ground, having tightened the wide band of truth (personal integrity, moral courage) around your waist and having put on the breastplate of righteousness (an upright heart).

Colossians 1:13-14 BSB

He has rescued us from the dominion of darkness and brought us into the kingdom of His beloved Son, in whom we have redemption, the forgiveness of sins.

Hebrews 13:20-21 AMP

Now may the God of peace [the source of serenity and spiritual well-being] who brought up from the dead our Lord Jesus, the great Shepherd of the sheep, through the blood that sealed and ratified the eternal covenant, equip you with every good thing to carry out His will and strengthen you [making you complete and perfect as you ought to be], accomplishing in us that which is pleasing in His sight, through Jesus Christ, to whom be the glory forever and ever. Amen.

_____
_____
_____
_____
_____
_____
_____
_____
_____
_____
_____
_____
_____
_____
_____
_____
_____
_____
_____
_____
_____
_____
_____
_____
_____

Equipped/ Commissioned with Authority

Mark 16:16-18 ESV

Whoever believes and is baptized will be saved, but whoever does not believe will be condemned. And these signs will accompany those who believe: in my name they will cast out demons; they will speak in new tongues; they will pick up serpents with their hands; and if they drink any deadly poison, it will not hurt them; they will lay their hands on the sick, and they will recover.

Matthew 10:1 KJV

And when he had called unto him his twelve disciples, he gave them power against unclean spirits, to cast them out, and to heal all manner of sickness and all manner of disease.

Matthew 28:19-20 KJV

Go ye therefore, and teach all nations, baptizing them in the name of the Father, and of the Son, and of the Holy Ghost: Teaching them to observe all things whatsoever I have commanded you: and, lo, I am with you always, even unto the end of the world. Amen.

Psalm 111:6 ESV

He has shown his people the power of his works, in giving them the inheritance of the nations.

Acts 3:6-7 NLT

But Peter said, "I don't have any silver or gold for you. But I'll give you what I have. In the name of Jesus Christ the Nazarene, get up and walk!" Then Peter took the lame man by the right hand and helped him up. And as he did, the man's feet and ankles were instantly healed and strengthened.

Acts 2:17-18 ESV

And in the last days it shall be, God declares, that I will pour out my Spirit on all flesh, and your sons and your daughters shall prophesy, and your young men shall see visions, and your old men shall dream dreams; even on my male servants and female servants in those days I will pour out my Spirit, and they shall prophesy.

Psalm 149:6-9 KJV

Let the high praises of God be in their mouth, and a two-edged sword in their hand; to execute vengeance upon the heathen, and punishments upon the people; to bind their kings with chains, and their nobles with fetters of iron; to execute upon them the judgment written: this honor have all his saints. Praise ye the LORD.

Do Not Fear

Psalm 118:5-6 KJV

I called upon the LORD in distress: the LORD answered me and set me in a large place. The LORD is on my side; I will not fear: what can man do unto me?

Psalm 112:6-8 BSB

Surely, he will never be shaken; the righteous man will be remembered forever. He does not fear bad news; his heart is steadfast, trusting in the LORD. His heart is assured; he does not fear until he looks in triumph on his foes.

_____

_____

_____

_____

_____

_____

_____

_____

_____

_____

_____

_____

_____

_____

_____

_____

_____

_____

_____

_____

_____

_____

Psalm 27:1-3 NIV

The LORD is my light and my salvation—whom shall I fear? The LORD is the stronghold of my life—of whom shall I be afraid? When the wicked advance against me to devour me, it is my enemies and my foes who will stumble and fall. Though an army besiege me, my heart will not fear; though war break out against me, even then I will be confident.

Psalm 46:1-3 ESV

God is our refuge and strength, a very present help in trouble. Therefore, we will not fear; though the earth gives way, though the mountains be moved into the heart of the sea, though its waters roar and foam, though the mountains tremble at its swelling. Selah.

Psalm 37:8-9 NIV

Refrain from anger and turn from wrath; do not fret—it leads only to evil. For those who are evil will be destroyed, but those who hope in the LORD will inherit the land.

Psalm 56:3-4 KJV

What time I am afraid, I will trust in thee. In God I will praise his word, in God I have put my trust; I will not fear what flesh can do unto me.

Psalm 56:8-11 NLT

You keep track of all my sorrows. You have collected all my tears in your bottle. You have recorded each one in your book. My enemies will retreat when I call to you for help. This I know: God is on my side! I praise God for what he has promised; yes, I praise the LORD for what he has promised. I trust in God, so why should I be afraid? What can mere mortals do to me?

Psalm 91:5-8 BSB

You will not fear the terror of the night, nor the arrow that flies by day, nor the pestilence that stalks in the darkness, nor the calamity that destroys at noon. Though a thousand may fall at your side, and ten thousand at your right hand, no harm will come near you. You will only see it with your eyes and witness the punishment of the wicked.

2 Timothy 1:7 KJV

For God hath not given us the spirit of fear; but of power, and of love, and of a sound mind.

Psalm 49:5-6 AMP

Why should I fear in the days of evil, when the wickedness of those who would betray me surrounds me [on every side], even those who trust in and rely on their wealth And boast of the abundance of their riches?

Philippians 1:28 AMP

And in no way be alarmed or intimidated [in anything] by your opponents, for such [constancy and fearlessness on your part] is a [clear] sign [a proof and a seal] for them of [their impending] destruction, but [a clear sign] for you of deliverance and salvation, and that too, from God.

Hebrews 13:6 KJV

So that we may boldly say, The Lord is my helper, and I will not fear what man shall do unto me.

_____

_____

_____

_____

_____

_____

_____

_____

_____

_____

_____

_____

_____

_____

_____

_____

_____

_____

_____

_____

_____

_____

_____

_____

Attitude of Trust in the Lord

Psalm 119:41-42 ESV

Let your steadfast love come to me, O LORD, your salvation according to your promise; then shall I have an answer for him who taunts me, for I trust in your word.

Psalm 118:8-9 NKJV

It is better to trust in the LORD Than to put confidence in man. It is better to trust in the LORD Than to put confidence in princes.

Psalm 118:29 ESV

Oh, give thanks to the LORD, for he is good; for his steadfast love endures forever!

Psalm 28:7 NLT

The LORD is my strength and shield. I trust him with all my heart. He helps me, and my heart is filled with joy. I burst out in songs of thanksgiving.

Psalm 9:9-10 ESV

The LORD is a stronghold for the oppressed, a stronghold in times of trouble. And those who know your name put their trust in you, for you, O LORD, have not forsaken those who seek you.

_____
_____
_____
_____
_____
_____
_____
_____
_____
_____
_____
_____
_____
_____
_____
_____
_____
_____
_____
_____
_____
_____
_____
_____

Psalm 7:1 KJV

O LORD my God, in thee do I put my trust; save me from all of them that persecute me, and deliver me.

Psalm 56:3 ESV

When I am afraid, I put my trust in you.

Psalm 34:22 ESV

The LORD redeems the life of his servants; none of those who take refuge in him will be condemned.

Psalm 37:39-40 NKJV

But the salvation of the righteous is from the LORD; He is their strength in the time of trouble. And the LORD shall help them and deliver them; He shall deliver them from the wicked, and save them, because they trust in Him.

Psalm 57:1-3 KJV

Be merciful unto me, O God, be merciful unto me: for my soul trusteth in thee: yea, in the shadow of thy wings will I make my refuge, until these calamities be overpast. I will cry unto God most high; unto God that performeth all things for me. He shall send from heaven, and save me from the reproach of him that would swallow me up. God shall send forth his mercy and his truth.

Psalm 112:6-8 NIV

Surely the righteous will never be shaken; they will be remembered forever. They will have no fear of bad news; their hearts are steadfast, trusting in the LORD. Their hearts are secure, they will have no fear; in the end, they will look in triumph on their foes.

2 Corinthians 1:10 NLT

And he did rescue us from mortal danger, and he will rescue us again. We have placed our confidence in him, and he will continue to rescue us.

Psalm 5:11-12 NKJV

But let all those rejoice who put their trust in You; let them ever shout for joy, because You defend them; let those also who love Your name be joyful in You. For You, O LORD, will bless the righteous; with favor, You will surround him as with a shield.

Attitude
of Victory

Romans 8:37-39 NKJV

Yet in all these things we are more than conquerors through Him who loved us. For I am persuaded that neither death nor life, nor angels, nor principalities nor powers, nor things present nor things to come, nor height nor depth, nor any other created thing, shall be able to separate us from the love of God which is in Christ Jesus our Lord.

Psalm 29:11 BSB

The LORD gives His people strength; the LORD blesses His people with peace.

_____

_____

_____

_____

_____

_____

_____

_____

_____

_____

_____

_____

_____

_____

_____

_____

_____

_____

_____

_____

_____

_____

_____

Psalm 66:3-4 NKJV

Say to God, "How awesome are Your works! Through the greatness of Your power Your enemies shall submit themselves to You. All the earth shall worship You And sing praises to You; They shall sing praises to Your name."

Psalm 66:8-9 NIV

Praise our God, all peoples, let the sound of his praise be heard; He has preserved our lives and kept our feet from slipping.

Psalm 68:19-20 KJV

Blessed be the Lord, who daily loadeth us with benefits, even the God of our salvation. Selah. He that is our God is the God of salvation; and unto GOD the Lord belong the issues from death.

Psalm 91:5-8 ESV

You will not fear the terror of the night, nor the arrow that flies by day, nor the pestilence that stalks in darkness, nor the destruction that wastes at noonday. A thousand may fall at your side, ten thousand at your right hand, but it will not come near you. You will only look with your eyes and see the recompense of the wicked.

Psalm 116:8-9 NIV

For you, LORD, have delivered me from death, my eyes from tears, my feet from stumbling, that I may walk before the LORD in the land of the living.

I Corinthians 15:56-57 NKJV

The sting of death is sin, and the strength of sin is the law. But thanks be to God, who gives us the victory through our Lord Jesus Christ.

Protection
of God

Psalm 18:16-17 NLT

He reached down from heaven and rescued me; he drew me out of deep waters. He rescued me from my powerful enemies, from those who hated me and were too strong for me.

Psalm 5:11-12 ESV

But let all who take refuge in you rejoice; let them ever sing for joy, and spread your protection over them, that those who love your name may exult in you. For you bless the righteous, O LORD; you cover him with favor as with a shield.

Psalm 31:3-5 KJV

For thou art my rock and my fortress; therefore, for thy name's sake, lead me and guide me. Pull me out of the net that they have laid privily for me: for thou art my strength. Into thine hand I commit my spirit: thou hast redeemed me, O LORD God of truth.

Psalm 31:19-20 NKJV

Oh, how great is Your goodness, which You have laid up for those who fear You, which You have prepared for those who trust in You In the presence of the sons of men! You shall hide them in the secret place of Your presence from the plots of man; You shall keep them secretly in a pavilion from the strife of tongues.

Psalm 32:7 KJV

Thou art my hiding place; thou shalt preserve me from trouble; thou shalt compass me about with songs of deliverance. Selah.

Psalm 37:12-13 NKJV

The wicked plots against the just, and gnashes at him with his teeth. The Lord laughs at him, for He sees that his day is coming.

Psalm 37:32-33 NIV

The wicked lie in wait for the righteous, intent on putting them to death; but the LORD will not leave them in the power of the wicked or let them be condemned when brought to trial.

Psalm 54:4-7 BSB

Surely God is my helper; the Lord is the sustainer of my soul. He will reward my enemies with evil. In Your faithfulness, destroy them. Freely I will sacrifice to You; I will praise Your name, O LORD, for it is good. For He has delivered me from every trouble, and my eyes have stared down my foes.

Psalm 59:8-10 BSB

But You, O LORD, laugh at them; You scoff at all the nations. I will keep watch for You, O my strength, because You, O God, are my fortress. My God of loving devotion will come to meet me; God will let me stare down my foes.

Psalm 62:1-2 NKJV

Truly my soul silently waits for God; from Him comes my salvation. He only is my rock and my salvation; He is my defense; I shall not be greatly moved.

Psalm 63:7-11 ESV

For you have been my help, and in the shadow of your wings I will sing for joy. My soul clings to you; your right hand upholds me. But those who seek to destroy my life shall go down into the depths of the earth; they shall be given over to the power of the sword; they shall be a portion for jackals. But the king shall rejoice in God; all who swear by him shall exult, for the mouths of liars will be stopped.

Psalm 71:2-3 KJV

Deliver me in thy righteousness, and cause me to escape: incline thine ear unto me, and save me. Be thou my strong habitation, whereunto I may continually resort: thou hast given commandment to save me; for thou art my rock and my fortress.

Psalm 109:21 ESV

But you, O GOD my Lord, deal on my behalf for your name's sake; because your steadfast love is good, deliver me!

Psalm 109:26-27 KJV

Help me, O LORD my God: O save me according to thy mercy: That they may know that this is thy hand; that thou, LORD, hast done it.

Psalm 127:1 ESV

Unless the LORD builds the house, those who build it labor in vain. Unless the LORD watches over the city, the watchman stays awake in vain.

Psalm 136:23-26 ESV

It is He who remembered us in our low estate, for his steadfast love endures forever; and rescued us from our foes, for His steadfast love endures forever; He who gives food to all flesh, for His steadfast love endures forever. Give thanks to the God of heaven, for His steadfast love endures forever.

Psalm 138:7 KJV

Though I walk in the midst of trouble, thou wilt revive me: thou shalt stretch forth thine hand against the wrath of mine enemies, and thy right hand shall save me.

Psalm 139:5 NLT

You go before me and follow me. You place your hand of blessing on my head.

Psalm 139:11-12 NKJV

If I say, "Surely the darkness shall fall on me," even the night shall be light about me; indeed, the darkness shall not hide from You. But the night shines as the day; the darkness and the light are both alike to You.

Psalm 140:7-8 KJV

O GOD the Lord, the strength of my salvation, thou hast covered my head in the day of battle. Grant not, O LORD, the desires of the wicked: further not his wicked device; lest they exalt themselves.

Psalm 141:8-10 BSB

But my eyes are fixed on You, O GOD the Lord. In You I seek refuge; do not leave my soul defenseless. Keep me from the snares they have laid for me, and from the lures of evildoers. Let the wicked fall into their own nets, while I pass by in safety.

Psalm 143:12 ESV

And in your steadfast love you will cut off my enemies, and you will destroy all the adversaries of my soul, for I am your servant.

2 Thessalonians 3:3 BSB

But the Lord is faithful, and He will strengthen you and guard you from the evil one.

Hebrews 2:18 NKJV

For in that He Himself has suffered, being tempted, He is able to aid those who are tempted.

Our Attitude from the Word

Psalm 119:65-66 BSB

You are good to Your servant, O LORD, according to Your word. Teach me good judgment and knowledge, for I believe in Your commandments.

Joshua 1:8 NKJV

This Book of the Law shall not depart from your mouth, but you shall meditate in it day and night, that you may observe to do according to all that is written in it. For then you will make your way prosperous, and then you will have good success.

Psalm 119:101-102 KJV

I have refrained my feet from every evil way, that I might keep thy word. I have not departed from thy judgments: for thou hast taught me.

Psalm 119:103-104 KJV

How sweet are thy words unto my taste! Yea, sweeter than honey to my mouth! Through thy precepts, I get understanding: therefore, I hate every false way.

Psalm 119:113-114 NKJV

I hate the double-minded, but I love Your law. You are my hiding place and my shield; I hope in Your word.

Psalm 119:157 NIV

Many are the foes who persecute me, but I have not turned from your statutes.

Psalm 119:161 NLT

Powerful people harass me without cause, but my heart trembles only at your word.

Psalm 119:41-42 ESV

Let your steadfast love come to me, O LORD, your salvation according to your promise; then shall I have an answer for him who taunts me, for I trust in your word.

Psalm 119:23-24 NIV

Though rulers sit together and slander me, your servant will meditate on your decrees. Your statutes are my delight; they are my counselors.

Psalm 119:49-52 KJV

Remember the word unto thy servant, upon which thou hast caused me to hope. This is my comfort in my affliction: for thy word hath quickened me. The proud have had me greatly in derision: yet have I not declined from thy law. I remembered thy judgments of old, O LORD; and have comforted myself.

Psalm 119:65 NKJV

You have dealt well with Your servant, O LORD, according to Your word.

Psalm 119:165 BSB

Abundant peace belongs to those who love Your law; nothing can make them stumble.

Authority of Jesus

Psalm 8:5-6 ESV

Yet you have made him a little lower than the heavenly beings and crowned him with glory and honor. You have given him dominion over the works of your hands; you have put all things under his feet,

Luke 4:36-37 BSB

All the people were overcome with amazement and asked one another, "What is this message? With authority and power, He commands the unclean spirits, and they come out!" And the news about Jesus spread throughout the surrounding region.

Matthew 28:18 ESV

And Jesus came and said to them, "All authority in heaven and on earth has been given to me."

Colossians 2:13-15 AMP

When you were dead in your sins and in the uncircumcision of your flesh (worldliness, manner of life), God made you alive together with Christ, having [freely] forgiven us all our sins, having canceled out the certificate of debt consisting of legal demands [which were in force] against us and which were hostile to us. And this certificate He has set aside and completely removed by nailing it to the cross. When He had disarmed the rulers and authorities [those supernatural forces of evil operating against us], He made a public example of them [exhibiting them as captives in His triumphal procession], having triumphed over them through the cross.

Hebrews 2:5-8 ESV

For it was not to angels that God subjected the world to come, of which we are speaking. It has been testified somewhere, "What is man, that you are mindful of him, or the son of man, that you care for him? You made him for a little while lower than the angels; you have crowned him with glory and honor, putting everything in subjection under his feet." Now, in putting everything in subjection to him, he left nothing outside his control. At present, we do not yet see everything in subjection to him.

James 1:13 NKJV

Let no one say when he is tempted, "I am tempted by God"; for God cannot be tempted by evil, nor does He Himself tempt anyone.

Jude 1:25 NLT

All glory to him who alone is God, our Savior through Jesus Christ our Lord. All glory, majesty, power, and authority are his before all time, and in the present, and beyond all time! Amen.

Acts 4:10 NKJV

Let it be known to you all, and to all the people of Israel, that by the name of Jesus Christ of Nazareth, whom you crucified, whom God raised from the dead, by Him this man stands here before you whole.

Galatians 1:3-4 ESV

...Jesus Christ, who gave himself for our sins to deliver us from the present evil age, according to the will of our God and Father.

Ephesians 1:21-22 KJV

Far above all principality, and power, and might, and dominion, and every name that is named, not only in this world, but also in that which is to come: And hath put all things under his feet and gave him to be the head over all things to the church.

Ephesians 4:9-10 NLT

Notice that it says "he ascended." This clearly means that Christ also descended to our lowly world. And the same one who descended is the one who ascended higher than all the heavens, so that he might fill the entire universe with himself.

Colossians 1:15-20 NLT

Christ is the visible image of the invisible God. He existed before anything was created and is supreme over all creation, for through him God created everything in the heavenly realms and on earth. He made the things we can see and the things we can't see—such as thrones, kingdoms, rulers, and authorities in the unseen world. Everything was created through him and for him. He existed before anything else, and he holds all creation together. Christ is also the head of the church, which is his body. He is the beginning, supreme over all who rise from the dead. So, he is first in everything. For God in all his fullness was pleased to live in Christ, and through Him God reconciled everything to himself. He made peace with everything in heaven and on earth by means of Christ's blood on the cross.

Colossians 2:9-10 NKJV

For in Him dwells all the fullness of the Godhead bodily, and you are complete in Him, who is the head of all principality and power.

Hebrews 1:3 AMP

The Son is the radiance and only expression of the glory of [our awesome] God [reflecting God's Shekinah glory, the Light-being, the brilliant light of the divine], and the exact representation and perfect imprint of His [Father's] essence, and upholding and maintaining and propelling all things [the entire physical and spiritual universe] by His powerful word [carrying the universe along to its predetermined goal]. When He [Himself and no other] had [by offering Himself on the cross as a sacrifice for sin] accomplished purification from sins and established our freedom from guilt, He sat down [revealing His completed work] at the right hand of the Majesty on high [revealing His Divine authority].

Belief:
The Power for
the Impossible

1 John 1:9 KJV

If we confess our sins, he is faithful and just to forgive us our sins, and to cleanse us from all unrighteousness.

John 14:14 NLT

Yes, ask me for anything in my name, and I will do it!

Romans 10:9-10 ESV

Because, If you confess with your mouth that Jesus is Lord and believe in your heart that God raised him from the dead, you will be saved. For with the heart one believes and is justified, and with the mouth one confesses and is saved.

Mark 11:23 KJV

For verily I say unto you, that whosoever shall say unto this mountain, Be thou removed, and be thou cast into the sea; and shall not doubt in his heart, but shall believe that those things which he saith shall come to pass; he shall have whatsoever he saith.

_____

_____

_____

_____

_____

_____

_____

_____

_____

_____

_____

_____

_____

_____

_____

_____

_____

_____

_____

_____

_____

_____

_____

_____

Mark 16:16-18 ESV

Whoever believes and is baptized will be saved, but whoever does not believe will be condemned. And these signs will accompany those who believe: in my name they will cast out demons; they will speak in new tongues; they will pick up serpents with their hands; and if they drink any deadly poison, it will not hurt them; they will lay their hands on the sick, and they will recover.

John 1:12 BSB

But to all who did receive Him, to those who believed in His name, He gave the right to become children of God.

John 14:12 KJV

Verily, verily, I say unto you, He that believeth on me, the works that I do shall he do also; and greater works than these shall he do; because I go unto my Father.

1 John 5:4-5 ESV

For everyone who has been born of God overcomes the world. And this is the victory that has overcome the world—our faith. Who is it that overcomes the world except the one who believes that Jesus is the Son of God?

1 John 5:13-14 NKJV

These things I have written to you who believe in the name of the Son of God, that you may know that you have eternal life and that you may continue to believe in the name of the Son of God. Now this is the confidence that we have in Him, that if we ask anything according to His will, He hears us.

Ephesians 1:19 ESV

And what is the immeasurable greatness of his power toward us who believe, according to the working of his great might.

Authority of the Word

Psalm 119:92-95 NKJV

Unless Your law had been my delight, I would then have perished in my affliction. I will never forget Your precepts, for by them You have given me life. I am Yours, save me; for I have sought Your precepts. The wicked wait for me to destroy me, but I will consider Your testimonies.

Psalm 119:153-154 NIV

Look on my suffering and deliver me, for I have not forgotten your law. Defend my cause and redeem me; preserve my life according to your promise.

Psalm 60:4-5 KJV

Thou hast given a banner to them that fear thee, that it may be displayed because of the truth. Selah. That thy beloved may be delivered; save with thy right hand and hear me.

Psalm 115:1 ESV

Not to us, O LORD, not to us, but to your name give glory, for the sake of your steadfast love and your faithfulness!

Psalm 119:170 NIV

May my supplication come before you; deliver me according to your promise.

1 Peter 1:13 ESV

Therefore, preparing your minds for action, and being sober-minded, set your hope fully on the grace that will be brought to you at the revelation of Jesus Christ.

1 John 2:14 AMP

I have written to you, fathers, because you know Him who has existed from the beginning. I have written to you, young men, because you are strong and vigorous, and the word of God remains [always] in you, and you have been victorious over the evil one [by accepting Jesus as Savior].

Psalm 143:9-10 NKJV

Deliver me, O LORD, from my enemies; in You I take shelter. Teach me to do Your will, for You are my God; Your Spirit is good. Lead me in the land of uprightness.

Colossians 3:15-17 BSB

Let the peace of Christ rule in your hearts, for to this you were called as members of one body. And be thankful. Let the word of Christ richly dwell within you as you teach and admonish one another with all wisdom, and as you sing psalms, hymns, and spiritual songs with gratitude in your hearts to God. And whatever you do, in word or deed, do it all in the name of the Lord Jesus, giving thanks to God the Father through Him.

Psalm 18:29-30 NKJV

For by You, I can run against a troop; by my God, I can leap over a wall. As for God, His way is perfect; the word of the LORD is proven; He is a shield to all who trust in Him.

Authority over the Enemy

Luke 10:19 AMP

Listen carefully: I have given you authority [that you now possess] to tread on serpents and scorpions, and [the ability to exercise authority] over all the power of the enemy (Satan); and nothing will [in any way] harm you.

Psalm 108:13 KJV

Through God we shall do valiantly: for He it is that shall tread down our enemies.

Psalm 9:3-4 ESV

When my enemies turn back, they stumble and perish before your presence. For you have maintained my just cause; you have sat on the throne, giving righteous judgment.

James 4:7 NKJV

Therefore, submit to God. Resist the devil and he will flee from you.

1 Peter 5:8-9 KJV

Be sober, be vigilant; because your adversary the devil, as a roaring lion, walketh about, seeking whom he may devour: Whom resist steadfast in the faith, knowing that the same afflictions are accomplished in your brethren that are in the world.

_____

_____

_____

_____

_____

_____

_____

_____

_____

_____

_____

_____

_____

_____

_____

_____

_____

_____

_____

_____

_____

_____

_____

_____

_____

Ephesians 6:10-12 AMP

In conclusion, be strong in the Lord [draw your strength from Him and be empowered through your union with Him] and in the power of His [boundless] might. Put on the full armor of God [for His precepts are like the splendid armor of a heavily-armed soldier], so that you may be able to [successfully] stand up against all the schemes and the strategies and the deceits of the devil. For our struggle is not against flesh and blood [contending only with physical opponents], but against the rulers, against the powers, against the world forces of this [present] darkness, against the spiritual forces of wickedness in the heavenly (supernatural) places.

Matthew 10:1 NKJV

And when He had called His twelve disciples to Him, He gave them power over unclean spirits, to cast them out, and to heal all kinds of sickness and all kinds of disease.

Matthew 18:18 ESV

Truly, I say to you, whatever you bind on earth shall be bound in heaven, and whatever you loose on earth shall be loosed in heaven.

Psalm 35:4-6 NKJV

Let those be put to shame and brought to dishonor who seek after my life; let those be turned back and brought to confusion who plot my hurt. Let them be like chaff before the wind, and let the angel of the LORD chase them. Let their way be dark and slippery and let the angel of the LORD pursue them.

Psalm 53:5 BSB

There they are, overwhelmed with dread, where there was nothing to fear. For God has scattered the bones of those who besieged you. You put them to shame, for God has despised them.

Psalm 60:12 ESV

With God we shall do valiantly; it is he who will tread down our foes.

Psalm 91:11-13 ESV

For he will command his angels concerning you to guard you in all your ways. On their hands they will bear you up, lest you strike your foot against a stone. You will tread on the lion and the adder; the young lion and the serpent you will trample underfoot.

Psalm 92:9-11 BSB

For surely Your enemies, O LORD, surely Your enemies will perish; all evildoers will be scattered. But You have exalted my horn like that of a wild ox; with fine oil I have been anointed. My eyes see the downfall of my enemies; my ears hear the wailing of my wicked foes.

Psalm 108:13 NLT

With God's help we will do mighty things, for he will trample down our foes.

1 John 4:4 KJV

Ye are of God, little children, and have overcome them; because greater is he that is in you, than he that is in the world.

Psalm 9:15-16 ESV

The nations have sunk into the pit that they made; in the net that they hid, their own foot has been caught. The LORD has made himself known; he has executed judgment; the wicked are snared in the work of their own hands. Selah.

Psalm 18:16-17 ESV

He sent from on high, he took me; he drew me out of many waters. He rescued me from my strong enemy and from those who hated me, for they were too mighty for me.

Attitude
of Prayer

Luke 11:9-10 NKJV

*So, I say to you, ask, and it will be given to you;
seek, and you will find; knock, and it will be
opened to you. For everyone who asks receives, and
he who seeks finds, and to him who knocks it will
be opened.*

Psalm 119:170 ESV

*Let my plea come before you; deliver me according
to your word.*

Psalm 3:4 ESV

I cried aloud to the LORD, and he answered me from his holy hill. Selah.

James 5:16 KJV

Confess your faults one to another, and pray one for another, that ye may be healed. The effectual fervent prayer of a righteous man availeth much.

Psalm 34:17-18 NIV

The righteous cry out, and the LORD hears them; He delivers them from all their troubles. The LORD is close to the brokenhearted and saves those who are crushed in spirit.

Psalm 50:14-15 ESV

Offer to God a sacrifice of thanksgiving, and perform your vows to the Most High, and call upon Me in the day of trouble; I will deliver you, and you shall glorify Me.

Psalm 55:16-19 KJV

As for me, I will call upon God; and the LORD shall save me. Evening, and morning, and at noon, will I pray, and cry aloud: and he shall hear my voice. He hath delivered my soul in peace from the battle that was against me: for there were many with me. God shall hear, and afflict them, even he that abideth of old. Selah. Because they have no changes, therefore they fear not God.

Psalm 91:15-16 BSB

When he calls out to Me, I will answer him; I will be with him in trouble. I will deliver him and honor him. With long life I will satisfy him and show him My salvation.

Psalm 118:5-6 NIV

When hard pressed, I cried to the LORD; he brought me into a spacious place. The LORD is with me; I will not be afraid. What can mere mortals do to me?

1 John 5:14-15 BSB

And this is the confidence that we have before Him: If we ask anything according to His will, He hears us. And if we know that He hears us in whatever we ask, we know that we already possess what we have asked of Him.

Psalm 120:1 NLT

I took my troubles to the LORD; I cried out to him, and he answered my prayer.

Receive Jesus as Your Savior

Choosing to receive Jesus Christ as your Lord and Savior is the most important decision you'll ever make!

God's Word promises, *"That if thou shalt confess with thy mouth the Lord Jesus, and shalt believe in thine heart that God hath raised him from the dead, thou shalt be saved. For with the heart man believeth unto righteousness; and with the mouth confession is made unto salvation"* (Rom. 10:9–10). *"For whosoever shall call upon the name of the Lord shall be saved"* (Rom. 10:13). By His grace, God has already done everything to provide salvation. Your part is simply to believe and receive.

Pray out loud: "Jesus, I confess that You are my Lord and Savior. I believe in my heart that God raised You from the dead. By faith in Your Word, I receive salvation now. Thank You for saving me."

The very moment you commit your life to Jesus Christ, the truth of His Word instantly comes to pass in your spirit. Now that you're born again, there's a brand-new you!

Receive the Holy Spirit

As His child, your loving heavenly Father wants to give you the supernatural power you need to live a new life. *"For every one that asketh receiveth; and he that seeketh findeth; and to him that knocketh it shall be opened…how much more shall your heavenly Father give the Holy Spirit to them that ask him?"* (Luke 11:10–13).

All you have to do is ask, believe, and receive!

Pray this: "Father, I recognize my need for Your power to live a new life. Please fill me with Your Holy Spirit. By faith, I receive it right now. Thank You for baptizing me. Holy Spirit, You are welcome in my life."

Congratulations! Now you're filled with God's supernatural power.

Some syllables from a language you don't recognize will rise up from your heart to your mouth (1 Cor. 14:14). As you speak them out loud by faith, you're releasing God's power from within and building yourself up in the spirit (1 Cor. 14:4). You can do this whenever and wherever you like.

It doesn't really matter whether you felt anything or not when you prayed to receive the Lord and His Spirit. If you believed in your heart that you received, then God's Word promises you did. *"Therefore I say unto you, What things soever ye desire, when ye pray, believe that ye receive them, and ye shall have them"* (Mark 11:24). God always honors His Word—believe it!

Please contact me and let me know that you've prayed to receive Jesus as your Savior or be filled with the Holy Spirit. I would like to rejoice with you and help you understand more fully what has taken place in your life. I'll send you a free gift that will help you understand and grow in your new relationship with the Lord.

Welcome to your new life!

Call for Prayer

If you need prayer for any reason, you can call our Prayer Line 24 hours a day, seven days a week at 719-635-1111. A trained prayer minister will answer your call and pray with you. Every day, we receive testimonies of healings and other miracles from our Prayer Line, and we are ministering God's nearly-too-good-to-be-true message of the Gospel to more people than ever. So I encourage you to call today!

CONTACT INFORMATION

Charis Bible College

800 Gospel Truth Way

Woodland Park, CO 80863

info@charisbiblecollege.org

Helpline Available 24/7: 719-635-1111

CharisBibleCollege.org

Also visit Carrie at: CarriePickett.com